I0797387

The Marriage Course Leaders' Guide, Revised and Updated

ISBN 978-0-310-11672-1 (softcover)
ISBN 978-0-310-09319-0 (ebook)

Requests for information should be sent to customercare@harpercollins.com

The Alpha name and trademarks are used under license from Alpha International.
Alpha USA, PO Box 7491, Carol Stream, IL 60197-7491

Published by HarperChristian Resources, a registered trademark of HarperCollins Christian Publishing, Inc.

First Printing 2020

The Marriage Course
Leaders' Guide

Contents

03

Welcome

Many years ago a government minister said to us, "We know that a strong society is built on strong families, and strong families are built on strong marriages. That's why we're interested in The Marriage Course."

We are so glad that you have decided to run The Marriage Course—to invest in marriages in your society and, in turn, invest in your own marriage. We hope you find the experience as enjoyable and rewarding as we do.

We've been running it three times a year since 1996, and we love it!

This Leaders' Guide is designed as a quick-reference guide to setting up and running your course. We find it helpful to have it with us when we are hosting a session. The checklists and timetables are particularly helpful for keeping us on track.

Please do let us know if you have any questions and do let us know how you get on.

Nicky and Sila

Nicky & Sila Lee

Creators of The Marriage Course

Introduction

The Marriage Course started at Holy Trinity Brompton (known as HTB), London, in 1996. Since then, it has been run in 127 countries around the world, reaching nearly one million couples.

The Marriage Course is an easy-to-run series of sessions designed to help couples invest in and strengthen their relationship. Some couples come to invest in an already strong relationship, others come to address specific challenges that they're facing. While based on Christian principles, The Marriage Course is designed for all couples, whether they have a faith background or not, and we welcome every couple whether they are married or cohabiting.

In 2020, The Marriage Course was updated and remade consisting of seven video episodes, hosted by Nicky and Sila Lee, featuring expert insights and drawing on the real experiences of couples from all over the globe. Courses run in a variety of venues and contexts, from churches and community centers to cafés and homes.

There are seven sessions in total. Each session starts with something to eat and drink—this helps to create a welcoming, romantic environment—followed by a talk and time for private conversations for each couple. Each guest is given a *Study Journal*, which provides guidance for each conversation and is an essential part of running the course.

For more information, please visit **alphausa.org/marriage** where you'll be able to watch training videos, access our latest resources, and register your course.

05

How to run

The Marriage Course is easy to run. We have a series of filmed episodes of the course content, which are available to buy and download on our website when you register a course.

Head to **alphausa.org/marriage** to download the episodes and make sure you buy enough *Study Journals* so guests have one each (two per couple—this is essential for doing the course) and get started.

Using the filmed episodes for your talks gives you time to focus on creating a welcoming, hospitable, and relaxing environment for your guests. Each episode includes content delivered by Nicky and Sila, as well as insights from leading experts and relevant stories from couples around the world.

There are clear prompts on the video when you need to pause to give couples time for a private conversation. These prompts match the guidance in the *Study Journal*. You'll also find the timings of these pauses for each session in the "Overview and session guide" section of this guide.

Everything you need to know about how to run the course is at your fingertips at **alphausa.org/marriage**.

06

Creating the experience

Creating a romantic, relaxing, and intimate atmosphere is an essential part of running The Marriage Course.

The welcome that couples receive and the atmosphere when they arrive will leave a lasting impression. Some couples may feel daunted and wonder whether they will be asked to share personal details about their relationship with others. Creating the right environment with the feel of an intimate date night will help to reassure them that the discussions they have will only be between the two of them.

This kind of atmosphere helps to create a safe space in which couples are more likely to open up and have meaningful conversations that are key to the course.

Venue

For a smaller course an ideal venue may be a home—this can be just like hosting friends. In this setting, you might choose to eat together first before separating as couples for the session's episode.

For a bigger course you will obviously need more space. This could be a church, a community center, or even a local restaurant or café.

Wherever you're hosting your course, you will need to be able to provide three things: something to eat and drink, a screen to watch the talk, and enough space to allow each couple to have their own private conversations.

Decor and lighting

The course should provide a relaxed space where guests feel like they're out on a date. If you have the space, individual tables for two will help create a feeling of intimacy and privacy. Candles, soft background music, low lighting, and flowers on the tables all help to set the right mood.

It's all about food

Every session starts with something to eat and drink. This helps guests to unwind from their day and is a chance for each couple to refocus on each other. What you choose to serve will vary depending on where you are in the world, the size of your course, and what time of day you're hosting it.

Serving dessert and tea and coffee when the couples are having their longest conversation helps to give guests the feeling that they've been hosted throughout the session.

If possible, it's a good idea to serve couples at their tables in order not to detract from the mood you've created.

Suggested room layout

Arrange separate tables for two sufficiently far apart to ensure each couple's conversations are private. Make sure everyone can see the screen and it's a good idea to allocate a space for guests to put their coats and bags.

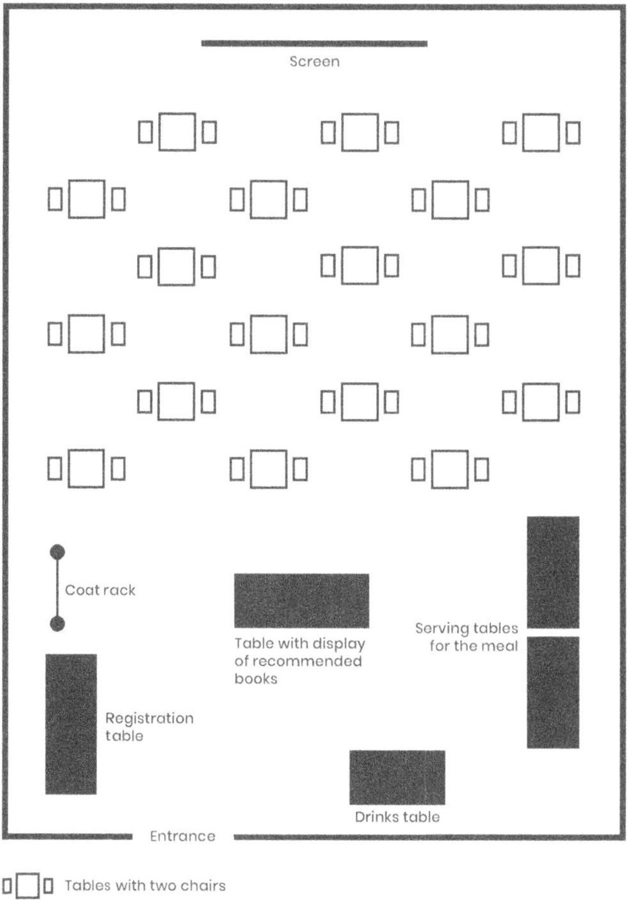

Screen

Coat rack

Table with display of recommended books

Serving tables for the meal

Registration table

Drinks table

Entrance

Tables with two chairs

09

Building a team

The Marriage Course is best run with a team. It's a great opportunity for people in the church to get involved, regardless of their life stage or relationship status. Depending on the size of your course, you will need enough volunteers to fill some, or all, of the following roles.

Course hosts

Course hosts usually open and close the evening and make announcements. They don't need to worry about giving talks as we recommend you use the video episodes to deliver all the course content. These are available on **alphausa.org/marriage** when you register your course.

Administrator

Your administrator will manage registration details, collect payments (if you are charging guests to help cover your costs), and ensure that all the resources you need are available for each session.

Room stylist

This person will use their skills to transform the venue into a special date night experience for the guests—where couples feel relaxed and can enjoy an evening out together.

Technical team

When this goes well, no one even notices there is an operator; but when it doesn't, everyone notices! The technical team runs the videos, plays background music, and displays any slides.

Caterer

Do you know someone who loves preparing food and may be willing to help with your course? If you're running a larger course, you could arrange an outside caterer to supply an affordable meal.

Welcomers and additional hosts

Making people feel welcome and relaxed as they arrive is essential. The welcomers will be the first people that guests meet, so try and think of the friendliest people you know and ask them to be part of the team.

For a larger course it's helpful to have additional hosts to help with welcoming, serving drinks, and being available to guests who may seek further support or advice.

Counseling support

Our experience is that around 10 percent of the couples on each course ask for additional support, some of whom need ongoing specialist help. Prepare for this with a referrals handout of local professional counselors.

Set up and pack down team

Depending on the size of your course, you might want to identify people who can help set up the venue for each session and pack it down afterwards.

Prayer team

Prayer is a vital aspect of running The Marriage Course. You could ask one person, or a team of people, to commit to praying for all the different aspects of your course—from the logistics, to the team and the guests.

11

Promoting your course

Most couples come on The Marriage Course because of a personal invitation. Telling others about your experience of the course helps to dispel the myth that The Marriage Course is only for couples who are struggling. The reality is that it's relevant for any couple wanting to invest in their relationship and make it stronger.

The following **six tips** will help to equip your team, members of your church, and couples who've already been on the course to tell others and invite them to your course.

12

01

Tell stories about your experience

What did you like and appreciate about the experience? What difference did it make to your relationship?

02

Explain that the course is for every couple

Whatever their situation—whether they are married or cohabiting, whether or not they are churchgoers, and whether their relationship is in good shape or they are struggling—The Marriage Course is for them.

03

Paint a picture of what the course looks like

Explain that it's like a date night—there's food and drink and a night off from the washing up. And reassure couples that they will not be asked to discuss anything about their relationship with anyone but their partner.

04

Give the date, time, and venue

As you approach the end of one course, it's helpful to have invitations for the next course printed and ready for guests to give out to their friends with their personal recommendation.

05

Spread the word

You can access a number of promotional resources online when you register a course. They include stories of relationships deeply impacted by the course as well as flyers, posters, and banners. Visit **alphausa.org/marriage**.

06

Register your course

Every time you run The Marriage Course, log in and register the details at **alphausa.org/marriage**. This will enable potential guests in your area to find it on our searchable map.

13

Common mistakes

We've identified six common mistakes and misconceptions that people have about The Marriage Course. We want to pass on what we've learnt over the years to help you run the best course possible.

"I have to have a perfect marriage to run the course"

Fear not, there is no perfect marriage! All you need is a desire to help others invest in their relationship. You certainly don't need to be a marriage expert—all the course content is available to download at **alphausa.org/marriage**.

"I need to adapt the course for my context"

The experience of thousands of hosts around the world is that the courses work in many, very different, cultures and contexts. Our encouragement is to keep to the basic course structure, content, and timing—we've found they work together to give couples the right amount of space to process what they are learning and to put it into practice.

Importantly, resist the temptation to add to or take away from the course material, to merge sessions, or extend or cut the conversation times.

"It's a course, so it should look like a classroom"

When the guests walk in, we don't want them to feel that they're attending a class or a lecture, or even a sermon; we want them to feel like they're on a date. A warm welcome and special atmosphere creates a feeling of safety and helps a couple to open up to each other and have those important, honest, and intimate conversations.

"Perhaps we should also do some group work..."

It's easy to think that it would be helpful for people to share what's going on in their relationship and to learn from each other's experiences. But couples come on The Marriage Course for a variety of reasons—knowing that the conversations are totally private and that there is no group work encourages many couples to attend who, otherwise, would not consider it.

"It's only for couples in our church"

The Marriage Course is for any couple, not just those in your church. It's actually a great way for the church to reach out and meet an important need in society. The course gives hope and encouragement, as well as practical tools, for any couple from any background, with or without a Christian faith.

"We've run it once, so now we're done"

In our experience, the majority of people who come on The Marriage Course do so because it has been recommended by someone who has found it helpful. The benefit of running multiple courses (two or three times per year, for example) is that it builds momentum and allows those who have completed the course to share their experiences and invite others to attend a future course.

In addition, we invite all the couples on The Pre-Marriage Course to come back to do The Marriage Course two years or so into their marriage. By this time they will be aware of the relevance of all the topics we address. Former guests on The Marriage Course are often interested in helping couples who are attending The Pre-Marriage Course by becoming a support couple and in the process continue to strengthen their own relationship. Having these two courses running in parallel on an ongoing basis provides a way of establishing and maintaining healthy marriages.

15

Session structure

Each session of your course will be about two-and-a-half hours long, including the meal. You can find specific timings for each session on pages 19–28. These follow the timings for our course in London, but you can adjust the start time depending on what is most suitable for your guests in your context.

Welcome

Some guests are apprehensive on the first evening; a warm welcome will help them relax.

The meal (30 minutes)

This enables you to nurture an atmosphere of a date for the couples and gives them time to reconnect.

Announcements and recap (up to 10 minutes)

After announcements, we provide couples with the opportunity to go back over what was covered in the previous session(s). Refer to the individual session guides, starting on page 19, for more details.

Episode and conversations (up to an hour and 45 minutes)

The episodes are interspersed with times for private conversation; these are opportunities for couples to talk together about an area of their relationship. The guidelines for these conversations are found in the *Study Journal* and generally last five to ten minutes, with one extended 30-minute conversation in each session. We recommend you play some background music to maintain the feeling of privacy for each couple.

The longer 30-minute conversation is a great time for the hosts and other volunteers to serve coffee or tea and some dessert, like a brownie or a slice of cake.

The timing of all the conversations will be indicated within each filmed episode and can also be found in the session guides, starting on page 19.

Conclusion

Each session in the *Study Journal* is followed by a section entitled "Continuing the conversation". This encourages guests to look at their calendars and plan in a date together in the coming week. There may be time for them to plan this before they go home at the end of the session.

At the start of the final session there are questionnaires available for guests to complete—these provide helpful feedback for next time around. You can find them when you register your course on **alphausa.org/marriage**.

17

Quick checklist

To make sure you're prepared and ready to go for your first session, we've put together a quick checklist of things you'll need to run the course and create a great atmosphere.

- ☐ This *Leaders' Guide*
- ☐ The Marriage Course episodes—purchase the DVDs or download the episodes at **alphausa.org/marriage** and register your course details.
- ☐ *Study Journals*—one per person
- ☐ TV screen or projector—to play the episodes
- ☐ Background music—to be played during the meal, the couples' conversations, and at the end of each session
- ☐ Catering: food and drink at the start and during the session
- ☐ Tables and chairs
- ☐ All the extra things to make the atmosphere special—suitable lighting, tablecloths, flowers and vases, candles, table napkins
- ☐ A list of guests who've registered for the course
- ☐ Pens—for guests to make notes in their journals
- ☐ Spare *Study Journals* to lend out in case any guests forget to bring theirs to a session
- ☐ Microphone—for larger groups
- ☐ Book stand—should you want to display any of the recommended reading
- ☐ End-of-course questionnaires for the final session only

18

19

Session Guide

Session 1
Strengthening Connection

Overview

This session helps couples to strengthen the connection between them by looking at what it takes to keep nurturing their relationship and by growing in their understanding of each other's emotional needs and desires.

Timetable

6:30 Be ready—guests often arrive early!

6:45 Welcome and drinks

6:50 Meal

7:15 Welcome

- Relax—you won't be asked to discuss anything about your relationship with anyone but your partner
- If you get stuck at any point on the course, please let us know. We or another couple would be very happy to see you privately. We also have details of a counsellor we could put you in touch with if necessary

7:25 Play **Episode 1 | Strengthening Connection**

7:31 Conversation 1: The first time you met **(5 minutes)**

7:50 Conversation 2: Working through challenges **(5 minutes)**

8:00 Conversation 3: Reviewing your connection **(30 minutes)**

8:40	Conversation 4: Special times together **(5 minutes)**
8:52	Conversation 5: Knowing me, knowing you **(10 minutes)**
9:05	End of session

Session 2

The Art of Communication

Overview

This session looks at the importance of communication within marriage—through talking and listening—and helps couples to identify and overcome barriers to effective communication, particularly any hindrances to listening to their partner.

Timetable

6:45 Welcome guests with a drink

6:50 Meal

7:15 Recap of Session 1

- (Optional) Briefly remind guests of the importance of spending quality time together and of recognizing each other's emotional needs and desires
- Encourage them to complete the "RECAP" section in the *Guest Journal*

7:25 Play **Episode 2 | The Art of Communication**

7:39 Conversation 1: A significant memory **(10 minutes)**

7:57 Conversation 2: Barriers to talking **(5 minutes)**

8:07 Conversation 3: The power of listening **(5 minutes)**

8:20 Conversation 4: Identifying bad habits **(5 minutes)**

8:37 Conversation 5: Reflective listening **(30 minutes)**

9:10 End of session

22

Session 3

Resolving Conflict

Overview

In this session, we look at how couples can increase their intimacy by expressing appreciation to each other, recognizing their differences, learning to negotiate disagreements, and supporting each other (either by praying together or by offering support in some other way).

Timetable

6:45 Welcome guests with a drink

6:50 Meal

7:15 Recap

- (Optional) Briefly remind guests of the power of listening effectively to each other and of the importance of seeking to meet each other's emotional needs
- Encourage them to complete the "RECAP" section in the *Guest Journal*

7:25 Play **Episode 3 | Resolving Conflict**

7:35 Conversation 1: Showing appreciation **(10 minutes)**

7:55 Conversation 2: Recognizing your differences **(10 minutes)**

8:25 Conversation 3: Using the five steps **(30 minutes)**

9:01 Conversation 4: Supporting each other **(5 minutes)**

9:07 End of session

Session 4

The Power of Forgiveness

Overview

This session addresses the ways we will inevitably hurt each other and how to resolve these issues. We look at the process of healing through talking about the hurt, saying sorry, and forgiving.

Timetable

6:45 Welcome guests with a drink

6:50 Meal

7:15 Recap

- (Optional) Briefly remind guests of the value of seeing our differences as complementary if we are to work effectively together as a team. Give an example from your own relationship (if applicable)
- Encourage them to complete the "RECAP" section in the *Guest Journal*

7:25 Play **Episode 4 | The Power of Forgiveness**

7:35 Conversation 1: Rhinos and hedgehogs **(5 minutes)**

7:44 Conversation 2: Handling anger **(15 minutes)**

8:17 Conversation 3: Identifying unresolved hurt **(30 minutes)**

8:57 Conversation 4: Comforting each other **(5 minutes)**

9:05 End of session

Session 5

The Impact of Family

Overview

This session focuses on helping couples to recognize how their family backgrounds affect the way they relate to each other. They also consider how to build a good, healthy relationship with their parents, in-laws, and wider family and how hurt from childhood can be healed.

Timetable

6:45 Welcome guests with a drink

6:50 Meal

7:15 Recap

- (Optional) Explain that the recap section covers the whole course so far. Point out that saying to our partner, "You're really good at..." and, "I need to work on..." are much more productive for our relationship than saying, "You need to work on..."
- Encourage them to complete the "RECAP" section in the *Guest Journal*

7:25 Play **Episode 5 | The Impact of Family**

7:40 Conversation 1: Current relationships **(10 minutes)**

7:57 Conversation 2: Supporting your parents **(10 minutes)**

8:21 Conversation 3: Reflecting on your upbringing **(30 minutes)**

9:02 Conversation 4: Comforting each other **(5 minutes)**

9:08 End of session

25

Session 6

Good Sex

Overview

Sex isn't just the icing on the cake of a marriage; it's a vital ingredient of the cake itself. In this session couples are encouraged to talk about their sexual relationship and to recognize where they could make changes for the sake of their partner and their whole relationship.

Timetable

6:45 Welcome guests with a drink

6:50 Meal

7:15 Recap

- (Optional) Remind guests of the need to set appropriate boundaries with parents, in-laws, and other members of their wider family so they are making their own decisions and supporting each other, while seeking to build the best relationships they can with family members
- Encourage them to complete the "RECAP" section in the *Guest Journal*

7:25 Play **Episode 6 | Good Sex**

7:40 Conversation 1: Understanding each other **(10 minutes)**

8:03 Conversation 2: Most romantic moments **(10 minutes)**

8:24 Conversation 3: Talking about sex **(30 minutes)**

9:04 Conversation 4: Supporting each other **(5 minutes)**

9:10 End of session

26

Remember to have your end-of-course questionnaires ready to give to guests at the final session next week. These can be found at **alphausa.org/marriage**.

Session 7

Love in Action

Overview

Drawing on the work of Dr. Gary Chapman, this session looks at five main ways of expressing and receiving love—through words, time, touch, presents, and actions. Couples discover which expression of love is most important for their partner and how they can put this into practice.

Checklist

- End-of-course questionnaires, which can be found at **alphausa.org/marriage**
- Invitations to your next Marriage Course

Timetable

6:45 Welcome guests with a drink

6:50 Meal

7:15 Notices and recap

- If you have your next course planned, make invitations available and encourage guests to invite their friends
- EITHER encourage guests to complete the "RECAP" section in the *Study Journal* OR invite them to complete the end-of-course questionnaire (explain that this will serve as a helpful recap of the whole course for them as well as being helpful to you to improve the experience of guests on future courses)

27

7:30	Play **Episode 7 | Love in Action**
7:50	Conversation 1: Favorite presents **(10 minutes)**
8:08	Conversation 2: Times together **(10 minutes)**
8:25	Conversation 3: Discovering your love languages **(30 minutes)**
9:02	Conversation 4: Supporting each other **(5 minutes)**
9:11	End of session

Ask guests to put any final comments on their end-of-course questionnaire and hand it in before they leave.

To purchase DVDs and study journals for The Marriage Course and The Pre-Marriage Course, visit **churchsource.com/collections/alpha-marriage**, or pay for digital access. For the first time ever, all the talks will be available to purchase online; while access to the updated training videos, introductory videos and downloadable Leaders' Guides will be available at no charge at **alphausa.org/marriage**.

Follow us on social media @marriagecourses

Alpha USA
P.O. Box 7491
Carol Stream, IL 60197-7491

800.362.5742

questions@alphausa.org
alphausa.org

@alphausa

Alpha Canada
#101-26 Fourth Street
New Westminister, BC V3L 5M4

800.743.0899

support@alphacanada.org
alphacanada.org

@alphacanada

Alpha in the Caribbean
Holy Trinity Brompton
Brompton Road
London SW7 1JA UK

+44 (0) 845.644.7544

americas@alpha.org
caribbean.alpha.org

@alphacaribbean

Pay It Forward

When more churches run Alpha, more guests meet Jesus. It's that simple. Alpha comes alongside the Church to train, equip, and provide effective resources to help them in their mission, all completely free of charge. We can do this because of your support in time, prayer, and donations. We are incredibly grateful for your partnership on this journey.

If you would like to help make this possible for more churches and guests to experience, you can give online at:

USA: alphausa.org/give | Canada: donate.alphacanada.org

www.ingramcontent.com/pod-product-compliance
Lightning Source LLC
Jackson TN
JSHW070115220726
105424JS00018B/174

9780310116721